WILDEST DREAMS

Words and Music by Taylor Swift

WILDEST DREAMS

Words and Music by
Taylor Swift, Max Martin and Shellback
Arranged by Duomo

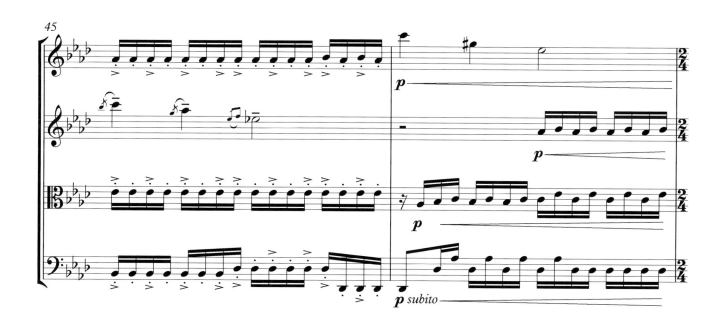

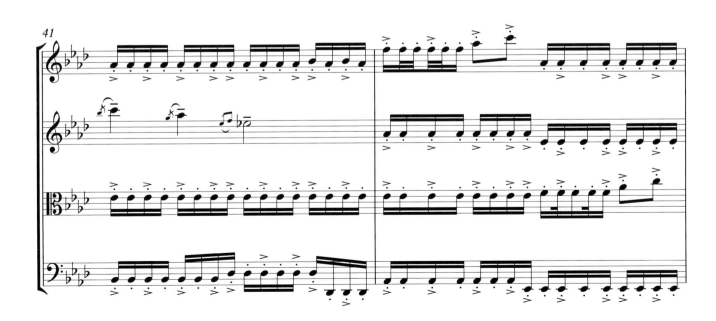

3

VIOLA

WILDEST DREAMS

Words and Music by
Taylor Swift, Max Martin and Shellback
Arranged by Duomo

2

WILDEST DREAMS

Words and Music by
Taylor Swift, Max Martin and Shellback
Arranged by Duomo

2